DUNGEONS
& TORTURE

BY
FIONA MacDONALD
AND DAVID SPENCE

WHAT IS A CRIME?

*E*very society, in every age, has had rules about good and bad behaviour. They have been passed on from elders to young people, or written down as laws. A crime is any action forbidden by these rules. It is often violent, and may cause death or injury. Crime can also damage whole communities, making members feel threatened, angry or insecure.

CRIMINAL DAMAGE

In many countries, damaging property is a serious offence. But for some people, it has become a way of making a political protest, or expressing their sense of hopelessness and frustration. For example, in parts of 20th century London, young people without homes or jobs, or who felt trapped by their addiction to drugs, deliberately damaged cars and shops belonging to wealthier members of the community. This photograph was taken during the Brixton riots of 1981.

MURDER MOST FOUL

Murder is the most serious crime anybody can commit. But it also fascinates millions of people, and songs, books, films and plays about murders are usually very popular. This poster was made to advertise a film made by British director Sir Alfred Hitchcock (1899-1980), who became famous for his violent crime "thrillers".

RIOTING

Today, most people in western democracies take the right to stage peaceful protests for granted. It was not always the same in the past. In 1819, a peaceful crowd of about 50,000 gathered in St Peter's Fields, Manchester, to campaign for parliamentary reform. The local magistrates sent soldiers to break up the demonstration, and 11 people were killed, and over 400 were injured.

BURGLARY

Dick Turpin (1705-1739) was an Essex butcher who joined the brutal, violent Gregory Gang. They broke into London houses after dark, terrorising the inhabitants.

THE KING'S BENCH

The King's Bench was an English court set up to deal with serious crime. In this 15th century manuscript, you can see royal judges dressed in red, lawyers holding legal documents, and shackled prisoners waiting for trial.

FRAUD & FORGERY

In the past, fraud and forgery were seen as very serious crimes. Criminals who made counterfeit banknotes or coins faced the death penalty. But by around 1800, many people thought this was too severe. One of them, cartoonist George Cruickshank (1792-1878) drew this mock banknote showing hanged forgers as a protest.

THE 'WEAKER SEX'?

Until the 20th century, women had to endure violence from their husbands or fathers. In England, the law allowed a man to beat his wife, so long as he did not break any bones.

Attacks on women by strangers were either ignored, or seen as the woman's fault. But in the 20th century, violence against women was recognised as a crime.

POACHING

In the past, poor people thought it was most unfair that rich, powerful people stopped them hunting wild animals for food on their land.

So, at nights, they went poaching (hunting illegally) to catch what they could. Soldiers also stole farm animals and wildlife as they marched through enemy land.

THIEVES & VAGABONDS

T here are many different reasons why crimes are commited – even for common offences like theft and burglary. Sometimes, the thief has no money, no home, or no work, and steals food or other essentials to survive. Sometimes they are envious of rich people, and steal because they want their share of good things. Sometimes, they choose to make a risky – but profitable - career out of crime. Until the 19th century, theft was punishable by death, but only violent or habitual thieves received this harsh sentence.

MOLL CUTPURSE

Mary Frith (1585-1660) was a well-known London thief. Tall and strong, she liked to dress as a man. Nicknamed 'Moll Cutpurse' or 'the Roaring Girle', she was sent to Newgate Prison (*see p.23*) for her crimes, but escaped by bribing the gaolers.

WHIPPED AT THE CART'S TAIL

England in the 16th century faced a social crisis. Many people were homeless and hungry, and could not find work. They felt angry about this, and wandered from town to town in gangs, threatening peaceful families. To combat these "sturdy beggars", governments introduced strict penalties. One involved being whipped and led through the streets, tied to a cart.

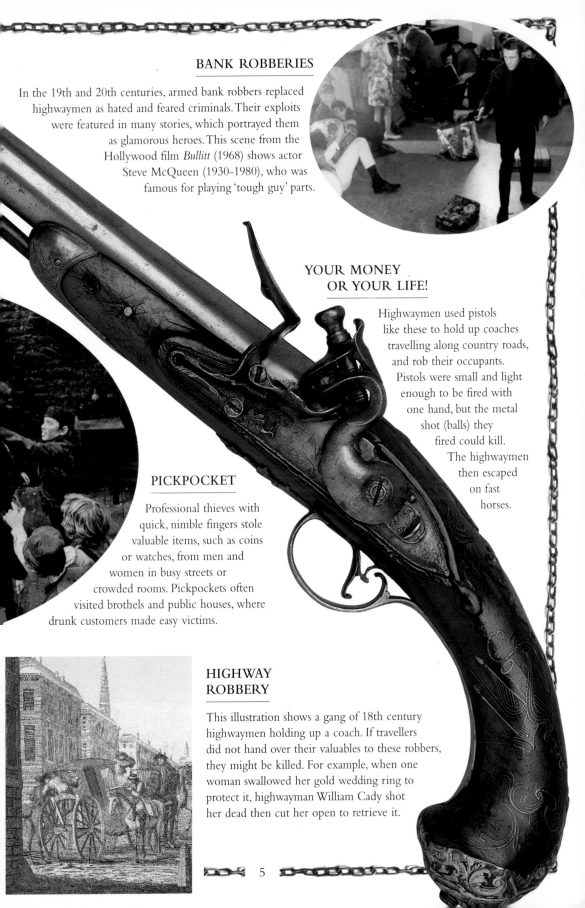

BANK ROBBERIES

In the 19th and 20th centuries, armed bank robbers replaced highwaymen as hated and feared criminals. Their exploits were featured in many stories, which portrayed them as glamorous heroes. This scene from the Hollywood film *Bullitt* (1968) shows actor Steve McQueen (1930-1980), who was famous for playing 'tough guy' parts.

YOUR MONEY OR YOUR LIFE!

Highwaymen used pistols like these to hold up coaches travelling along country roads, and rob their occupants. Pistols were small and light enough to be fired with one hand, but the metal shot (balls) they fired could kill. The highwaymen then escaped on fast horses.

PICKPOCKET

Professional thieves with quick, nimble fingers stole valuable items, such as coins or watches, from men and women in busy streets or crowded rooms. Pickpockets often visited brothels and public houses, where drunk customers made easy victims.

HIGHWAY ROBBERY

This illustration shows a gang of 18th century highwaymen holding up a coach. If travellers did not hand over their valuables to these robbers, they might be killed. For example, when one woman swallowed her gold wedding ring to protect it, highwayman William Cady shot her dead then cut her open to retrieve it.

WAR CRIMES & POLITICAL VICTIMS

CAPTIVES FOR RANSOM

This painting shows prisoners captured in war. Bound, blindfolded, and almost naked, they are being paraded before a victorious king. Wealthy prisoners were set free once they paid a large ransom. Poor prisoners, who could not pay, were often killed.

*L*aws are made by people with power who claim to be acting for the good of the whole community. In wars, or times of political upheaval, however, the normal rules of law are often ignored. In the past, invading armies robbed and raped civilians, and victorious kings murdered their enemies. Some players in this brutal "game" of politics were cruel and manipulative, committing any crime that was necessary to stay in power.

VIOLENT PROTEST, VIOLENT PUNISHMENT

In Britain, campaigners for women's right to vote were known as the Suffragettes. They smashed windows, set fire to mail-boxes, and chained themselves to public buildings to draw attention to their cause. Many were arrested and sent to prison, where they went on hunger strike. Prison guards force-fed them, brutally pushing feeding tubes down into their stomachs. The Suffragette leader, Emmeline Pankhurst (1858-1928), was violently force-fed 12 times.

GOD'S JUDGEMENT?

During the British Civil Wars (1639-1660) troops supporting Parliament, led by general Oliver Cromwell, savagely massacred civilians and soldiers at Drogheda and Wexford in Ireland. They also ruthlessly executed leaders of the Levellers, a group of radical English politicians. Cromwell was a deeply religious man, and felt that his war crimes were approved by God as a punishment for his enemies' wickedness.

CHURCH OR STATE?

Thomas Becket (c1120-1170) was a clever lawyer, and the trusted friend of King Henry II of England. But after he became Archbishop of Canterbury, he supported the Church in fierce political quarrels with the king. Henry felt betrayed, and very angry. He urged his followers to get rid of "this meddlesome priest". Four of the king's knights hurried to Canterbury, where they found Becket in the cathedral. They killed him as he knelt in prayer.

VICTIM OR VILLAIN?

Charles I of England (reigned 1625-1649) was a good man, but a hopeless king. His quarrels with Parliament led to the Civil War. Parliament won, and its leaders put Charles on trial. He was found guilty, condemned to death, and executed. After his head was cut off, many Londoners queued to dip their handkerchiefs in his blood. They believed it was holy, because he had been unjustly killed.

ROYAL CONSPIRACY

Mary Queen of Scots (1552-1587) was headstrong and emotional. She married English nobleman Henry Darnley, although her advisors disapproved. But Mary soon stopped loving him, and spent time with her secretary, David Riccio. Darnley was jealous, and had Riccio murdered.

RELIGIOUS CRIMES

RELIGION & POLITICS

In 1605, soldier Guy Fawkes plotted to blow up the Houses of Parliament in London, using barrels of gunpowder. He was a Roman Catholic, and at that time, Catholic worship was against the law. Fawkes hoped to kill the king, as a protest. But he was captured and tortured, then hung, drawn and quartered, along with all the other men involved in the plot. Ever since then, English people have lit bonfires, let off fireworks and burned "guys" (lifelike models) on 5th November, to commemorate the Gunpowder Plot.

*U*ntil the 20th century, religion was a powerful force in most peoples' lives. It brought hope and comfort, and promised them a place in heaven after death if they obeyed religious laws. These laws set standards for personal behaviour, banning lying, cheating and sex outside marriage, as well as public crimes, such as murder. But they also tried to control what people thought or believed. People with strange or controversial beliefs were condemned as heretics or witches, and savagely punished as dangerous criminals.

SUFFERING IN HELL

People who broke religious laws feared that they would be sent to Hell after they died. This illustration from a medieval manuscript shows people in Hell being punished for the sin of envy. Cruel demons, armed with pitchforks, are continually moving them between tanks of boiling and freezing water.

DEATH BY FIRE

In most parts of Europe, being burnt alive was the punishment for witchcraft. Thousands of women – and some men – were put to death this way. Their killers hoped to destroy every bit of their bodies, so no dangerous fragments would remain. The first known witch to be burned was Angela of Labarthe, in France, in 1275, and burnings continued until the 18th century. But in England witches were hanged, and burning was reserved for heretics – people with wrongful or dangerous religious beliefs.

HOLY LAWS

The Bible tells how Jewish leader Moses led the Hebrews out of Egypt, towards the Promised Land. At the start of this long journey, God gave Moses Ten Commandments, written on two slabs of stone. For almost 3,000 years, these Commandments laid down rules of good behaviour in many parts of Europe and the Middle East. Today, they are honoured by Jewish and Christian people worldwide.

PRIVATE LIVES

This manuscript illustration, made around AD 1200, shows a priest (centre) separating a German husband and wife. Church laws did not allow divorce, so neither would be permitted ever to marry again. The wife has custody of their child. She also holds some shears, representing her share of the family property.

CONDEMNED BY THE KING

Many rulers resented the Church's power to make laws that governed their own behaviour. In 1536, King Henry VIII gave orders for monasteries in England and Wales to be dissolved (shut down). He claimed that the monks were lazy and corrupt. But really, he wanted to take over their lands, as part of his quarrel with their spiritual leader, the Pope in Rome.

SHAME & MOCKERY

*I*n the past, penalties for wrong-doing were often severe, even for minor offences. They were designed to express the community's anger, and its contempt for the criminal. They also aimed to discourage other people from committing crimes. Many punishments for minor crimes were based on public humiliation. This was especially important when most people lived in small communities, surrounded by families and close friends. Although the punishment might not hurt them physically, it caused them great mental distress. It also damaged their reputation for ever.

IN DISGRACE!

Men and women who cheated their friends and neighbours, or refused to pay what they owed, might be shamed into handing over money by this punishment. A large notice, with a "D" for "Debtor" was hung round their necks, and they were paraded through the streets on busy market days. This not only shamed them, but warned others that they could not be trusted.

SHAMEFUL SIGN

"Respectable" women were meant to behave quietly and modestly in public. They were also expected to cover their hair. These 18th century women have been accused of leading rowdy, immoral lives. As a punishment, their heads have been shaved. People hoped this would destroy their beauty, and its power to 'lead men astray'.

A SUITABLE PUNISHMENT?

Some punishments were specially invented to fit the crime. This drunken man, pictured here in an 18th century print, has been forced to walk through the streets wearing only a heavy beer-barrel. By the end of his walk, he will be shivering, smelly, bruised – and very ashamed.

DUCKING STOOL

The ducking stool was another way of punishing women accused of being gossipy and disagreeable. They were tied to a close-stool (chair fitted with a chamber-pot) and repeatedly dipped into the nearest river or pond. This punishment was last used in England in 1809.

A Scold's Bridle

HOLD YOUR TONGUE!

The Scold's Bridle (named after part of a horse's harness) was a metal cage used to punish women accused of scolding (excessively nagging) their families or spreading harmful gossip. It had a metal spike that fitted into the woman's mouth and stopped her speaking or even moving her tongue. A rope or a chain was fitted to the bridle so that she could be led through the streets in disgrace.

LAUGHING STOCK

Minor criminals, like shopkeepers who sold stale food, were shut in the stocks – a wooden frame that trapped the hands and legs. Passers-by jeered at them, and pelted them with mud, rotten vegetables or horse-dung.

CRUEL PUNISHMENTS

For many centuries, punishments for most crimes were very severe. They often inflicted great pain, and left offenders permanently disabled. Based on the Bible teaching "an eye for an eye, a tooth for a tooth", they aimed to make the criminal suffer as badly – or worse – than their victim had done. Cruel punishments were usually carried out in public, often in front of large crowds, as a warning to the rest of the community.

CAT-O'-NINE TAILS

This whip, made of wood, rope and leather, had nine separate strands, designed to inflict maximum pain with each blow. Each strand is tipped with a tight, hard knot, designed to cut into the flesh like a cat's claws. Whips like this were used in all the British armed forces, and were not abolished until 1948.

BRANDED!

Branding involved the use of a red-hot iron to mark someone with a letter or sign. Vagabonds (wandering beggars) were often branded with a 'V' on the cheek or hand. In 1630, one controversial preacher was branded on the face with 'SS' (Sower of Sedition, an old term for disobedience) for criticising the king. He also had his nose slit and his ears cut off, and was flogged before being shut up in prison for life!

THE BOOT

If people accused of crimes refused to confess their guilt, or name their accomplices, an iron boot might be used to punish their "crime" of stubbornness. It was clamped round their lower leg, while wooden wedges were hammered into it. These crushed the flesh and bones inside, causing terrible pain.

NAVY DISCIPLINE

Good discipline was vital on board warships, especially when long voyages kept sailors away from land for several months at a time. They might easily get depressed, rebellious or simply bored. But some Navy punishments were savage. This 19th-century engraving shows a British sailor being whipped for disobeying orders, while all his shipmates look on.

IN THE PILLORY

The pillory was a wooden frame that locked around the head and hands. It was used to punish minor crimes, but its effects could sometimes be serious. The criminal trapped inside was unable to protect his head or face from sticks and stones thrown by passers-by, and might be badly injured.

TRANSPORTATION

One way of reducing crime was to expel criminals from the country. From the 17th century onwards, the British government "transported" men and women convicted of serious crimes to distant parts of the world. If they returned home, they were killed. The most famous convict settlement was at Botany Bay, in Australia. The first British transport ships arrived there in 1778, with about 775 convicts on board. Convicts had to work in gangs for the British rulers of Australia. They cleared land, built houses, loaded ships, and served free settlers. Transportation finally ended in 1867.

HUMAN TRADE

From 1614 onwards, the British government paid contractors to transport convicts to North America and the Caribbean. When the convicts reached America, they were sold as "indentured labourers" – workers who were bound by law to serve their masters for up to fourteen years.

ON GUARD

Patrols of Royal Navy vessels like these smart, fast frigates, were used to guard convoys of ships loaded with British convicts on their way to Australia. Their journey of 15 thousand miles across dangerous oceans took almost nine months to complete. Conditions on board the ship were harsh, and many convicts did not survive.

CONVICT TOWN

Although life in Botany Bay was hard, future prospects for the families of convicts were good. Within 20 years, the children of convicts became known as 'cornstalks'. They had grown to be much taller than their parents, because of the warm climate and plentiful food.

RACE RELATIONS

This noticeboard carries a very clear message – equal justice for all! It was put up on the orders of Sir George Arthur, the British Lieutenant General of Van Diemen's Land (Tasmania) in 1828. It was designed for Aboriginal people, and for British convicts who could not read.

KANGAROO ISLAND

Kangaroo Island (main picture) is situated off the east coast of Australia. It became a retreat for "white pirates", convicts who had escaped from prison colonies in Australia to live as outlaws. These men captured local Aboriginal people, and forced them to work as slaves.

GONE FOREVER

This 19th-century book illustration is poking fun at criminals about to be separated from their families. It shows two sisters weeping as their brother is about to be led on board a convict ship. The pair know they might never see him again.

CAPITAL PUNISHMENT

*T*oday, many people think that killing criminals is a cruel and unnecessary punishment, however wicked their crime. Past societies thought differently, however. By the 18th century in England, there were hundreds of offences that carried the death penalty, from stealing a sheep to plotting to kill the king, but juries often refused to convict people accused of minor, non-violent crimes. Criminals could also apply for "Benefit of Clergy". If they could prove that they could read (the test piece was usually Psalm 51), offenders were set free. Executions were grim and grisly, but very popular as entertainment. Thousands of men, women and children gathered to watch criminals die at sites like the Tyburn gallows in London (now known as Marble Arch).

HANGMAN'S NOOSE

Hanging was a terrible way to die. Until scaffolds with trapdoors were invented, the "drop" did not always break a criminal's neck. It might take several agonising minutes before they died from choking or suffocation. When this happened, relatives or friends sometimes hung on to the writhing body, hoping their extra weight would hasten the death.

LAST JOURNEY

Criminals sentenced to death were carried in carts to places of execution – usually open fields on the edge of large towns. Often, they were forced to wear the shroud they would be buried in or sit next to their own coffin. A priest read prayers to them as they travelled along. The last public hanging in Britain took place in 1868.

BEHEADING

Noblemen and women could claim the "privilege" of having their heads chopped off, rather than being hanged. This was a much quicker, less painful, way to die. There were two methods. In England, condemned men and women knelt on the ground, and rested their head on a block of wood while the executioner wielded an axe. In France and Germany, as shown here, heads were chopped off with the swing of a sword.

FIRING SQUAD

Soldiers and sailors who mutinied might be sentenced to death by firing squad. The bullets that killed them were fired by their former comrades, all at the same time, so that no man would know who had fired the fatal shot.

DEATH SWEAT

Superstitious people believed that the touch of a hanged man's hands had the power to heal. They even climbed up onto the scaffold to collect drops of sweat from the dead body.

A KIND WAY TO DIE?

The guillotine kills people by cutting off their heads with a very sharp knife. It was named after a French doctor, Joseph-Ignace Guillotin (1738-1814). He did not invent the contraption – similar machines had been used elsewhere in Europe before – but Guillotin persuaded the French government to use it at executions. He hoped to reduce each criminal's suffering by making the death-blow as swift and complete as possible.

DISMAL DUNGEONS

DYING IN GAOL

Few people in the past were sentenced to life imprisonment, but many died in gaol. They were killed by cold, damp and dirt, or by dangerous diseases carried by rats and fleas. Some were poisoned by their gaolers; or deliberately neglected, to die from hunger and thirst. A few simply died of despair.

In the past, prison was not seen as a place of punishment. Instead, it was a safe stronghold to keep suspects awaiting trial, and other people who might disturb the community, such as political protesters, debtors or war captives. They were put in prison to wait (sometimes for months or years) until the judges arrived to investigate their case. All people in prison had to look after themselves. No food, drink or furniture was provided. Prisoners relied on friends to send in supplies. If this didn't happen, they starved. A few prisoners managed to find ways of earning money. Tailors imprisoned in London, for example, sat sewing in their cells. Others used their time in captivity to write books, or, like Mary Queen of Scots, to embroider huge wall-hangings.

WORDS OF COMFORT

The Church taught that it was a Christian duty to visit people in prison, and to help them. Many believers ignored this, saying that prisoners had brought their misfortunes on themselves by breaking the law. But a few dedicated priests preached and said prayers in gaol, and prison reformers like Quaker Elizabeth Fry (1780-1845) were inspired by Christian ideas to campaign for better conditions.

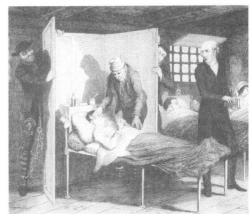

IN IRONS

Some prisoners were chained to prison walls or floors, for extra security. But this did not always succeed. In 1724, notorious robber Jack Sheppard was imprisoned in Newgate gaol in London. In just three hours, he escaped. He was re-captured, and locked in the securest part of the prison, with his legs in chains and his wrists in handcuffs. Amazingly, Sheppard escaped again. His adventures inspired many popular plays and songs.

PRISON HULK

Old rotting ships (known as hulks) were moored at ports and used as temporary prisons. Conditions inside were much worse than ordinary gaols. Hulks housed many prisoners of war, and also convicts awaiting transportation to America and Australia.

THE BLOODY TOWER

RAVENS

A flock of ravens – birds who feed on carrion (dead flesh) have lived at the Tower of London for centuries. Legends tell how London will face disaster if they ever leave.

*T*he Tower of London has a fearsome reputation. "In truth, there is no sadder spot on earth," wrote the famous nineteenth century historian, Thomas Macaulay. The Tower has witnessed many deaths, tortures and executions in the long years since it was built by William the Conqueror soon after 1066.

TOWER HILL

Public executions took place on the hill just outside the Tower. Only very important prisoners were allowed to be executed privately, within the walls. This print shows the public execution of two Jacobite nobles, Lord Balemerino and Lord Kilmarnock, in 1746. They had rebelled against King George III. During the execution, one of the stands overlooking the scaffold collapsed, crushing several people to death.

ANNE BOLYEN

A beautiful and fascinating young noblewoman, Anne Boleyn (1501-1536) became King Henry VIII's second wife. But when she failed to produce a son and heir, Henry sent her to the Tower of London, accusing her of adultery. She was tried, convicted and beheaded.

PRINCES IN THE TOWER

In 1483, boy-king Edward V and his younger brother were kidnapped and imprisoned in the Tower of London. Soon afterwards, their uncle, Richard of York, proclaimed himself king, as Richard III (reigned 1583-1485). The princes were never seen again, and many people blamed Richard for their murder. In 1674, the skeletons of two young boys were found near the White Tower. They were taken to Westminster Abbey and given a Christian burial.

THE WHITE TOWER

Over the years, many walls, gateways, bastions and smaller towers have been built around the great central keep of the Tower of London. This became known as the White Tower, because it was built on a mound known as "White Hill" - not because of its colour! In fact, the keep's walls look pale red, because they contain crushed Roman bricks and floor tiles.

LONDON LOCK-UPS

*L*ondon has always been the biggest city in England, and a great centre of crime. Because of this it has many prisons. Newgate, the best-known, housed common criminals. The Fleet, Clink, and Marshalsea prisons were for debtors, while Bedlam contained people who were mentally ill. The Tower of London was used to lock up political prisoners or members of noble families.

GOING HUNGRY

Tradesmen visited London prisons, offering food, drink, and other luxuries for sale to prisoners who could afford them. If a prisoner had no money, he or she went hungry. Prison guards were also bribed to smuggle prostitutes into gaol, to entertain male prisoners.

PRIVILEGED PRISONERS

Debtors were locked up in the Fleet prison until they paid back what they owed. Since debt was a civil, not a criminal offence, prisoners in the Fleet were free to work, receive visitors or even to get married. Many had their wives and children living with them, because their families had nowhere else to go.

BEDLAM

The Bethlehem Royal Hospital, a former monastery, was converted into a 'lunatic asylum' (a secure hospital for people with mental illness) in 1547. It was meant to be a place of safety for dangerous or vulnerable people, but soon became a popular tourist attraction. Its name became used as a word meaning 'madhouse'.

HUMAN ZOO

As late as the 1820s, it was possible to visit Bedlam hospital for a fee and stare at unhappy prisoners sitting in a trance or behaving in a bizarre manner. Those who objected were taken away and punished or put into solitary confinement. Thankfully, this freak show finally died out in the 1860s, although the institutions stayed open well into the 20th century.

THE BLACK PEW

Monday was the day for executions in Newgate gaol. On the previous Sunday, prisoners sentenced to death were taken to the prison chapel, and made to sit in the "black pew" around a coffin, and listen to the "condemned sermon". Sightseers paid to watch them from the public gallery.

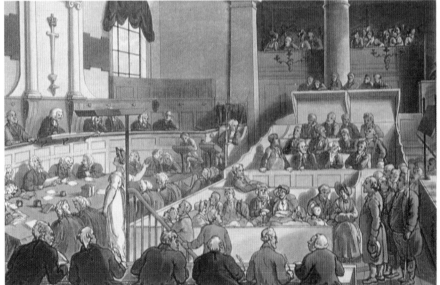

HOUSES OF CORRECTION

ON THE TREADMILL

This illustration shows prisoners walking the treadmill. The treadmill was a machine rather like a hamster's exercise wheel, that was designed to occupy their time, exhaust their bodies and get them used to working hard. It was deliberately made uncomfortable to use, to punish prisoners and deter them from offending again.

*I*n the past, many people believed that criminals had "bad blood", and were destined to lead evil lives. But others did not agree. They set up "houses of correction", where petty criminals, or "nuisances" such as beggars who refused to find jobs, were locked up and forced to labour at pointless or unpleasant tasks. The authorities hoped this would re-educate prisoners, and turn them into law-abiding workers. These ideas were copied in ordinary prisons, and in "workhouses" – miserable buildings where men and women too old or ill to look after themselves were given food and lodging, but treated like prisoners.

INNOCENT PRISONERS

Until the 19th century, each parish community had a duty to look after its own poor. Wandering beggars and homeless people were locked up in houses of correction, until they could be sent home, even though, by modern standards, they had committed no crime. This 18th-century print shows the "pass-room" at the London Bridewell, where miserable females were confined for 7 days before being sent to their respective parishes.

CHILDREN IN GAOL

The most famous house of correction was the Bridewell prison, in London, in use from 1553-1855. Mothers sent there had to take their children with them if they had no family or friends who could care for them outside. Some women also became pregnant in prisons, since male and female prisoners were locked up together.

LOCKS & BARS

Houses of correction could be just as grim as any other prison. Governors used many devices to try and stop prisoners escaping, like these locks, bolts, spikes and bars.

BEATING HEMP

Men and women in houses of correction were often given tiring, dirty jobs to do, such as beating hemp. This involved hitting the tough stalks of hemp plants with a heavy mallet to extract the stringy, prickly fibres they contained. These fibres were then twisted together to make rope.

HARD LABOUR

Gangs of prisoners were sometimes let out of gaol and forced to work on government building projects, such as new Navy dockyards at Woolwich, in London. They were chained together to stop them running away, and forbidden to speak to passers-by.

THUMBSCREW

This device was often used by the Inquisition – a team of investigators employed by the Roman Catholic Church to hunt down witches and heretics. The victim's fingers or thumbs were held in a trap, and slowly crushed between two iron bars that moved closer together as a screw on the trap was turned.

EXTRACTING CONFESSIONS

*C*ourts in past times used many cruel methods to extract confessions from suspects, or to try to prove their guilt or innocence. These included torture and ordeals. Torture was officially banned in England in 1641, but everywhere, prison governors and guards, soldiers, witch-finders and even Church investigators used violence against suspects and prisoners. Torture was mostly used to get evidence, or to force prisoners to plead guilty. But sometimes it backfired, and prisoners being tortured died from their injuries before they could be brought to trial.

DEADLY EVIDENCE

The ordeal of "bier right" or "bier proof" was based on the ancient superstition that a dead body had the power to convict the person who killed it. The person suspected of murder was stripped naked, tied by a rope around the waist, then led to the place where a dead body lay on its bier (coffin frame). Then they were made to touch the body's wounds. If these bled, the suspect was guilty.

WATER TORTURE

Water torture could be physical or psychological. For physical torture, water was poured down the victim's throat, filling his stomach and, eventually, his lungs. For psychological torture, the victim was shut up alone in a darkened room, and forced to listen to the steady "drip, drip" of water for days and nights on end. Alternatively, water was slowly dripped onto a prisoner's forehead for several days.

RACK

The rack was a large timber frame, raised above the ground, with rollers at each end. The victim's hands were tied to one roller, and their feet to the other. Then the rollers were turned in opposite directions, tearing their muscles and ligaments, dislocating their joints and causing serious internal injuries. All this caused excruciating pain. With luck, the victim soon became unconscious.

TEST OF INNOCENCE?

Ducking (or swimming) was an ordeal designed to prove guilt or innocence. The suspect, usually a woman accused of witchcraft, was cross-bound, with her right toe tied to her left thumb, and her right thumb tied to her left toe. Then she was dipped or thrown into a pond. If she floated, she was guilty. If she sank, she was innocent – but dead!

WITCHFINDERS

Eccentric, unhappy or unpopular old women were often accused of witchcraft. Special investigators, know as witchfinders, used torture to force them to confess. Popular methods included sleep deprivation, burning the soles of the feet, pouring boiling fat over their bodies, or hanging them from the ceiling by their hands.

TERRIBLE ENDS

Gaolers and executioners invented many horrible ways of killing criminals and of making them suffer before they died. Traitors were particularly harshly punished. They were sentenced to "hanging, drawing and quartering". They were hanged, then, while they were still alive, their intestines and genitals were removed, and burned before their eyes. Finally their remains were hacked into four quarters, and their head was chopped off.

PEINE FORT ET DURE

The name of this strange torture is French for "severe and hard punishment". It was used to kill prisoners who refused to answer accusations made against them. The victim was taken to a low dark room, and placed on the floor in a spread-eagled position. Heavy objects were placed on their chest, eventually crushing them to death.

BLOWING IN THE WIND

The bodies of criminals executed for particularly violent crimes might be hung in gibbets (iron cages) at crossroads or other public places until only the bones remained. This gibbet still contains the skull of murderer John Breads, executed in the town of Rye, in Sussex, in 1742.

DRAWN ASUNDER

A particularly horrible punishment was reserved for criminals who attacked kings and queens. For example, the man convicted of trying to kill King Henri IV of France (reigned 1589-1610) was tied to horses, and then pulled apart.

SEVERED HEADS

The heads of executed criminals were often placed on spikes lining London Bridge, the main thoroughfare linking north and south London. This macabre display gave a sombre message to passers-by. No matter how rich or powerful the criminal had once been, after death, they were nothing more than rotting flesh and bones.

SOLD FOR STUDY

The bodies of condemned criminals were often sold to doctors, who cut them up to find out how different organs worked, or to study the effects of disease. Society in those days saw this as a really terrible punishment. It meant that people punished in this way could not "rise from the dead" to enjoy eternal life after Judgement Day.

ROAST IN HELL

This medieval manuscript illustration shows dead criminals being thrown by demons into the fire of Hell. Once there, their bodies would suffer anguish eternally, without ever being burnt up by the fire. Many criminals made confessions of all their sins, and asked for the Church's forgiveness, before they died. They hoped to avoid hell-fires this way.

PROTECTION & DETECTION

*U*ntil the 19th century, there was no national police force in most European countries. Instead all adult were responsible for maintaining law and order in their own communities. They organised themselves into vigilante groups, or paid guards called watchmen to look after their property. The 19th century also saw a new, scientific study of crime. Professors and politicians puzzled over what caused criminal behaviour, and how best to prevent it, questions which still concern us today.

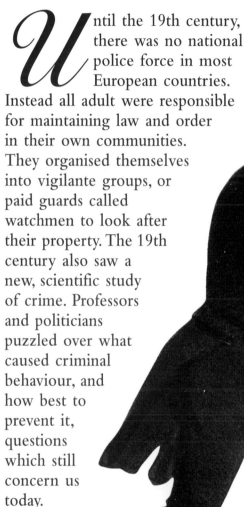

CRIMINAL SIGNATURE

No two people have identical skin patterns on their fingertips. For centuries, investigators in China and Japan used fingerprints as a way of identifying criminals. In 1892, Sir Francis Dalton pioneered their use in Britain.

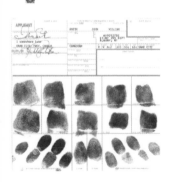

PEELERS

In 1929, Home Secretary Sir Robert Peel recruited a new police force for London. These men wore uniforms to make them easy to recognise as they walked through the streets, and were based in small district stations, so they would get to know the local community. They were nicknamed "Bobbies" or "Peelers".

THE NIGHT WATCH

Before 1800, most villages and towns employed night watchmen – untrained security guards who patrolled the streets after dark and guarded locked gates in city walls. In some cities, they also had to call out time every hour.

THE SCIENCE OF CRIME

In the 19th century, scientists began to study criminals, to see if they could find any physical or mental differences between them and law-abiding people. They weighed and measured prisoners and questioned them closely, hoping to identify a special "criminal type". Some went further, and argued that convicted criminals should be banned from having children, so that they would not pass their "criminal genes" on to the next generation.

PRIVATE PROTECTION

Until state-sponsored policemen were introduced early in the 19th century, rich people paid private bodyguards to protect themselves and their property. This was especially necessary when they travelled outside their homes, due to the threat of highwaymen and robbers. Poor people, who could not afford to pay for such protection, often fell victim to criminal gangs.

A GLOSSARY OF INTERESTING TERMS

Bent - Criminal or corrupt, the opposite of "straight", which means honest or true.

Blood money - Fee paid for information leading to the arrest of a murderer.

Cat burglar - Criminal who climbs silently into a house, like a cat.

Clean hands - Freedom from guilt.

Clean sheet - Having no record of any past offences.

Crack a crib - To break into a house and steal something.

Darbies handcuffs - Named after Father Darby, a 16th-century money-lender who made very strict agreements with his clients to force them to pay back the money they had borrowed.

Fall guy - Criminal's victim. The word comes from rigged wrestling matches, where the loser fell and was badly beaten.

Gaol fever - Disease (probably typhus, carried by lice) that killed many prisoners, prison warders and lawyers.

Grass - Criminal or criminal's accomplice who give information to the police. From Cockney rhyming slang "grasshopper" = "copper" = "policeman".

Hand of glory - Hand of a hanged criminal, soaked in oil and used by witches, who believed it to have magic powers.

Hue and cry - System of catching criminals, dating from Anglo-Saxon times. When any villager called for help to catch a criminal, by shouting or blowing his hunting horn, all the neighbours had the duty to assist him.

Nobble - To arrest.

Peterman - Criminal skilled at breaking into safes. The term comes from the use of "peter" as a name for a safe or strongbox.

Posse - Group of armed men working to enforce the law. From the Latin word "posse" to be able.

Prickers - 17th-century Scottish witch-hunters. At that time, people believed that witches could not feel the pricking of pins. Prickers "tested" suspects, to see how they reacted to pain.

Put the finger on - To accuse someone of a crime.

Put the screws on - To put pressure on someone to make them give in to demands. Refers to the use of thumbscrews to extract money or confessions.

Resurrectionists - Criminals who stole newly-dead bodies from graveyards, and sold them to doctors to cut up and study. Also called "body-snatchers".

Screw - Prison warder. From the word "turnscrew", because the earliest locks on prison doors fastened with screws, not keys.

Sin-eater - Someone who ate bread or salt placed on top of the coffin of a dead person. By doing so, they were believed to "eat up" the deceased's sins and save him or her from punishment in Hell.

Stool pigeon - Police spy or informer. From the habit of tying a tame pigeon to a roost, to attract wild pigeons which hunters would shoot.

Swag - Stolen goods. From the Viking word "to swing" = a bag of stolen goods swing over the shoulder.

Tea-leaf - Thief, from Cockney rhyming slang.

Watch and Ward - From the 13th century, the duty of each township in England to keep a 24-hour lookout for robbers and rioters.

ACKNOWLEDGEMENTS

We would also like to thank: Graham Rich and Elizabeth Wiggans for their assistance
Printed in Egypt. Copyright © 2003 ticktock Entertainment Ltd.
No part of this publication may be reproduced, stored in a retrieval system, or transmitted in any form or by any means, electronic, mechanical, photocopying, recording or otherwise, without prior written permission of the copyright owner.
A CIP Catalogue for this book is available from the British Library. ISBN 1 86007 414 6